IT'S TIME TO LEARN ABOUT COLLIE DOGS

It's Time to Learn about Collie Dogs

Walter the Educator

Silent King Books
A WhichHead Entertainment Imprint

Copyright © 2025 by Walter the Educator

All rights reserved. No part of this book may be reproduced in any manner whatsoever without written per- mission except in the case of brief quotations embodied in critical articles and reviews.

First Printing, 2024

Disclaimer

This book is a literary work; the story is not about specific persons, locations, situations, and/or circumstances unless mentioned in a historical context. Any resemblance to real persons, locations, situations, and/or circumstances is coincidental. This book is for entertainment and informational purposes only. The author and publisher offer this information without warranties expressed or implied. No matter the grounds, neither the author nor the publisher will be accountable for any losses, injuries, or other damages caused by the reader's use of this book. The use of this book acknowledges an understanding and acceptance of this disclaimer.

It's Time to Learn about Collie Dogs is a collectible early learning book by Walter the Educator suitable for all ages belonging to Walter the Educator's Time to Eat Book Series. Collect more books at WaltertheEducator.com

USE THE EXTRA SPACE TO TAKE NOTES AND DOCUMENT YOUR MEMORIES

COLLIE DOGS

The Collie dog is kind and smart,

It's Time to Learn about Collie Dogs

With gentle eyes and loving heart.

It watches, guards, and plays with glee

A loyal friend for you and me!

Its fur can be both long and thick,

With colors that you get to pick!

From sable, black, or white and gray,

It shines and sways in breeze all day.

With pointed nose and ears held high,

It spots a squirrel racing by!

Its senses sharp, its steps are quick

The Collie's moves are smooth and slick.

It started out on farms with sheep,

To guard the flock and never sleep.

It herded them from hill to pen,

And back again, then back again!

It's Time to Learn about
Collie Dogs

The Collie listens very well,

It learns commands and stories tell.

"Sit," "stay," and "fetch" are fun to do

This pup is smart, and helpful too!

It's gentle with the little ones,

It plays along and joins the fun.

It watches over babies near,

And gives them kisses ear to ear.

The Collie loves to run and race,

It dashes through an open space.

But when it's done, it'll rest beside,

With head on lap and sleepy pride.

Some Collies star in books and shows,

Like Lassie, who just always knows!

A hero dog with heart so true,

It's Time to Learn about
Collie Dogs

That saves the day and helps you too.

To care for Collies, brush their coat,

And keep them clean from tail to throat.

They like good food, a walk each day,

And lots of hugs along the way.

So if you meet a Collie pup,

Be kind, and stop, and kneel down up.

You'll find a friend so brave and true

It's Time to Learn about
Collie Dogs

A Collie just might choose you!

ABOUT THE CREATOR

Walter the Educator is one of the pseudonyms for Walter Anderson. Formally educated in Chemistry, Business, and Education, he is an educator, an author, a diverse entrepreneur, and he is the son of a disabled war veteran. "Walter the Educator" shares his time between educating and creating. He holds interests and owns several creative projects that entertain, enlighten, enhance, and educate, hoping to inspire and motivate you. Follow, find new works, and stay up to date with Walter the Educator™

at WaltertheEducator.com

www.ingramcontent.com/pod-product-compliance
Lightning Source LLC
LaVergne TN
LVHW051920060526
838201LV00060B/4095